A Splash
of Cave Paint

Marc Vincenz

SPUYTEN DUYVIL
NEW YORK CITY

Printed in the United States of America

for Ibices and sierras

ARTIFICAL EVIDENCE ACCUMULATES

Ay & Ay Ay
Space, the Final Frontier
Tinman Poem
Alternate Worlds
The Cartographer
The Biologist's Husband
Artificial Intelligence

TABULA RASA

Doctor Mel Blanc in the House
Perhaps
An Empire in the Ground
An Epitaph for Someone Alone in the
Ground
An Expressionist Painting on Mars
A Splash of Cave Paint
Alien Nation
An Aftervoyage
Sudden Sheen of Thought
The Castle of Forbidden Language
The Castle of Public Knowledge

ALL ROADS LEAD TO LHASA

Part One – {Plastique}

I. Tai Pan Chinese Restaurant Behind Rosemont
II. Martha's Haberdashery on Humboldt Circle Five
III. How To Skin a Weasel Twenty-One Ways
Splayed
Constrained
Folding & Unfolding
Wednesday Morning
Bespoke Corduroy
To Be Outdone
A Primal Response
Have a Dram on Me
Forgive Me
A Sun in Any Another Galaxy
Always in the City
A Number
Fly in the Ointment
Upturned
Greasy Holy Water
Undisturbed
On the Order of Twelve Dozen
On the Deck of an Ocean Liner
From the Armchair
After the Age of Innocence
After the Tea Party

Part Two – {All These Flat Surfaces}

≈

A lizard, a Spanish gecko dances ...

On a Beach Somewhere in Tibet
A Primitive State
A Less Primitive State
"Don't Forget Where You Came From
Imagining a Dystopian Future
Eye-Roll
Something Else Emerges from the Primordial Soup

ARTIFICAL
EVIDENCE
ACCUMULATES

The hallway smothered in iodine.

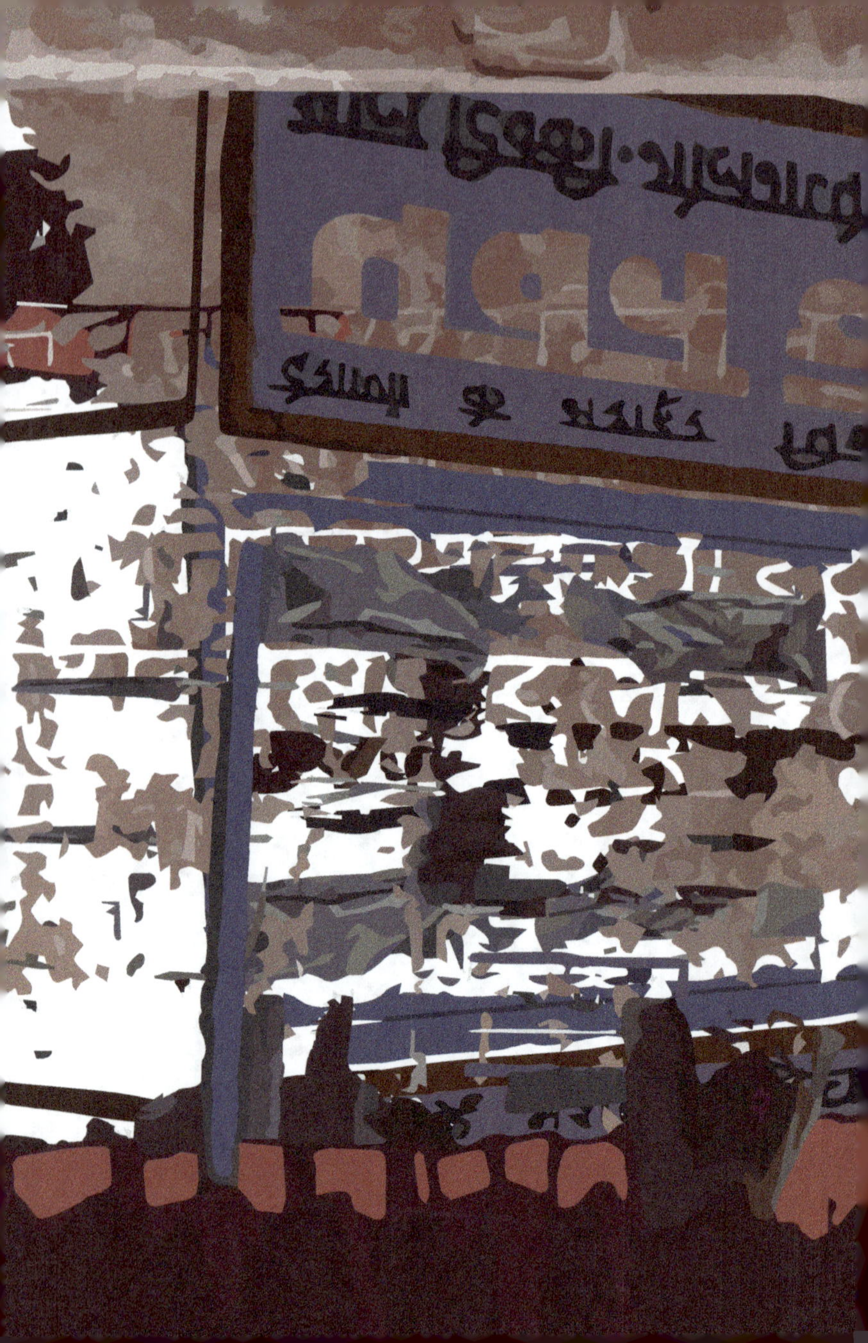

Ay & Ay Ay

With worms for fingers
And snails for eyes,
The mad world could refuse
Me no answer, when
For the just cause
My corpse was deeply moved.
And in that late hair of mine,
An entire forest root-system,
The first man started to walk.
Should I dare speak
Of the metaphor
Behind the metaphor?
O, how I wish to be
A café in Paris
Spooning chocolate mousse
Into your mouth, then
Smoking Gauloises
With a piccolo of champagne.
The waiter too
Has snails for eyes
And a chestnut tree of hair.
I'll say it again, as if
I've never said it:
The prophets wait
For the dark end of days.

Space, the Final Frontier

Or in

the storm

of the vac u m?

"Have a

m o d i c u m

of decency,"

said she.

"It means

an entirety,

and

there's

p l e n t y ."

Tinman Poem

On the chalkboard, Tinman squeaks.
I see stars in his chalklines,
Worlds in his cloud of chalkdust,
Raising archaic symbols
In his fine fingerwork.

(My neighbor believes it has all happened before, a thousand times or more, and we are simply the latest seed, an experiment, one fancy in the line of many, all built within the process of elimination. [He's fabricated himself a basement within a basement just in case.])

At night, Tinman repeatedly tells me:
"The mountain speaks balderdash."
And then, "Can you see your old garden from here?"

"Without falter," I say.
"Well, do you hear what she says?"
"She moves in her own way,
Crossing bricks and cement and stones,
Reclaiming all her lost bones."
"Denouncing us," says Tinman.

Alternate Worlds

I.

"Are all about the ability to see," says she, even on her space-walks by the pool, she who knows the vacuum of space with its view of the stars; she who thought she new the ingredients of reality itself.

She knows there is nothing bigger than the cosmos.

Hell, she could grab it by the scruff of its neck, that apprentice experience of space.

II.

"It was like a broadband beam of signals," the alien said.

In her interrogation, the detective said, "She stonewalled just about everything."

The second, a man with mutton chops in his forties, said: "The cat's in the bag, sir."

III.

She, in her demeanor, soured by the grapes she had just devoured, said: "To hell with all this official procedure! Scoundrels each and every one of you! The prophets died off long ago!"

Hell-bent, with my heart folded in the road, I said: "In everything there is a virtue."

They all laughed, raised their beers, and toasted on the spot what fortuitous lot had brought us here.

The Cartographer

for Thomas Seach

I.

As battered as a proverb, he trudges his way
Down the mountain. A word falls into his head,
Something like *scruple*, or was it *purple*? Last
Night he saw zigzags in the darkness above his bed,

Then there was that shooting star that earned him
The name Cosmic Tom. He's run out of water, so
He's still sucking cough drops. At two thousand feet
He feels analgesic, but then, unfurling from

The eaves of the forest, a peacock appears.
"My wife," he says to the bird, "my wife whose eyes
Are the equal of water." Down below, beneath those
Vertical chalk cliffs, the manta rays are gathering

In the turquoise ocean; up here,
                              the birds and the trees
Are playing their swansong. Breath regained, he

Edges his way toward the seabreeze.
Salt hits the back of his throat.
The peacock makes him sneeze.

II.

Third month in these gorges; the bamboo rats,
The thatch huts and their occupants estranged to me;

Mother with two children and a dog; lone fisherman
With an extremely long fishing pole and a tin bucket;

Starfish in unexpected places: between the soles
Of your shoes, crawling across your chest in the dead

Of night; and that water canister undeniably
Low. Now dusk burns yellow and a line appears

In his mind, as if the Buddha himself, or God,
Had come to him: "See your original nature!"

Someone says, "All those grand human affairs weigh
The same and leave foul memories." Outside

Limestone and chalk and granite are gathering
To conspire the world he made of stone.

The Biologist's Husband

Looking for his voice, he rounds the corner and finds the hallway smothered in iodine. He hears the squeak of unknown rodents, the hoot of an owl, perhaps? He remembers again how the Malaysian jungle left him bare. Each day he had less strength. Once they laid out his body in the sun in a grove where the crows were singing something like "Santo Ignacio!" all day long. And then, at the end, a single crow roared, "I will not see it! I will not see it!"

In his eyes, the ribbons of tears that formed planets coalesced and he knew he was born from a star or a stone; nothing more was ever uttered.

Artificial Intelligence

They say the autumn
Will come with white sails.
My mouth is always wide
Open to praise.

Eternal youth is a gift
From all that brings joy,
The clouds or the gods.
With a sweet tension,

They lighten the load.
"How can there be
Bad love?" you say.
"It all vanishes

In dust and smoke," you say.
"Even those pressure pads
Leave something in doubt;
In no uncertain words,

The olive trees have seen
Most of your eras, your
Changing of the guard,
Your wax seals and notary

Publics, with your digital
Signatures and a fannypack
Of tricks, with your theatres
And organic bistros.

I wish I had a daughter
Whose name was Esmeralda
Or Josephina, a landscape
Of diversity to survey;

A pledge, a ledge
To lean upon,
Or a mantel, or a lintel;
And that Friday

Night when pines turn
Into palm trees ...

Honestly, I'd prefer
To circle the earth,

And consider
Which one

Of these galaxies
Will soon be singing."

TABULA RASA

Sometimes I loved her too,
but her autumn leaves
always revived my soul.

Doctor Mel Blanc in the House

Untinted or tinged, un-
Touched and un-
Fingerprinted,

No skin or feather cells,
The Y chromosome may
Actually be missing—

Or something else; in an earth
Without wind?
Who collects the leaves?

You must realize this.
Nothing—and yet we
Tremble. Perhaps

We ought to sleep
This off? Yeah,
What's up Doc?

Perhaps

Every re-

ality, in,

as it does,

concern it-

self with its

own self, ex-

ists only

with-

in the shadow

of its own-

dreamed

self.

An Empire in the Ground

Linen stretching mound to mound,
The heat of the day passes through the ceiling.

A row of soldiers. The cold air plucks at threads.
Manikins here and there, washed in soap and lavender;

A weasel creeps into the picture with fish in her teeth.
Useful, they say, eons away. We shall have our crest

Of arms. Don't all armaments need alms?
My friend says (at least I think it's him), adjusting

His gas mask. His filter needs to be changed,
His eyes and thyroid are running out; surely

The blood-sugar levels too, wiping away
Any trace of what came before.

Somewhere in this rubble
A mouse is fishing for stale bread.

An Epitaph for Someone Alone in the Ground

Be heartened, dear soul,
With all your colors flying

Your spirit will hasten
To its eternal end, toward

The foothills and as far
As the eye can see; here

It rains apricots and
Every night is a Ramadan.

Everything smells of almonds,
Red wine and vinegar,

Of garlic and mint,
Of black tea and nicotine.

Tarry along, as they say
In the old country, I have

One red apple saved
For you, my heart.

An Expressionist Painting on Mars

Every night you call
>The doctor; I think

>>That's what caused
>>>My angina, what

>>>Caused the factory
>>>>To go on strike,

What caused that
>*Personne célèbre* to slink

>>Into the dark.
>>Either way,

>>It's a lot to put
>>On one person's shoulders.

Enlist the doctor,
>You say? Really? As if ...

>>And yet the light tonight
>>Is all a swirl in it-

>>Self. Bring out the wine,
>>I say. Let us listen to that old

Melody, let us toss dead
>Leaves to the w i n d.

A Splash of Cave Paint

"Count the dots, Jackson Pollock."
So said the shaman to her daughter
While braiding her hair.

Alien Nation

Out of the city they come with their telescopes and their spokes of the third kind. Remember that year I was thrown inside?

I repeat, what I wrote on the walls at that time have forsaken me; if we have a myth to carry us through, one that's good enough to suggest there's dozens of surprises. For example, that chain for killing snakes, the red stone that owns your home, the three faculties of the human species: intellect and will in moderation; that moral duty to be civil, respectful, age-appropriate; and that other viscera not tied up in a nose or a face or eyes; like any animal, tied up in the early phase, the secrets carried through the valleys, over the hills, the obviousness of everything. How you're never fooling yourself, how it carries on its obliviousness; how each jail is a treasury and each frozen road the transparent sleeve of a dream.

Tell me, how many times have we orbited this sun?

An Aftervoyage

Glazed walls growing seaweed; a different game
than turning a goat into a mouse; of course the
night is starry-eyed. Sometimes I loved her too,
but her autumn leaves always revived my soul.

Yes, yes, she said. Follow the River of the Dead
until you reach a brick wall, then you need to
get suited up, scuba suit, oxygen tank; deep
in the lower shaft, beneath the kelp forms,
through the ribbons of damp violets, through
the Passage of the Reeds, past the sacred texts
scrawled by schoolboys on their way to Saint
Ignatius; feel the leather in your shoes and the
linen on your skin; then, without remorse face
that gilded statue of a woman and child, and
call out into the dark, call out into the light.

There are things that make you want to confuse
things. I can't recall, was it my grandmother
who said *Namaste*? Or was it the voice of a tree
roving in my ear?

Sudden Sheen of Thought

The sum of things is surely worth more than you imagined; in all of its conspiring, a modicum of appreciation. How could we be so single-minded when we lived among the roots?

For months we had been carrying those severed souls; all this consciousness in our hands.

This is a sure thought: there are no survivors, all heroes come to an end. It's just the relatives of the giving who never give up. Through all these ruins, you still search your pocket for a fluff of something, a scrap of evidence.

You reach in, find a lock of hair, some pencil shavings, a brand-new notebook.

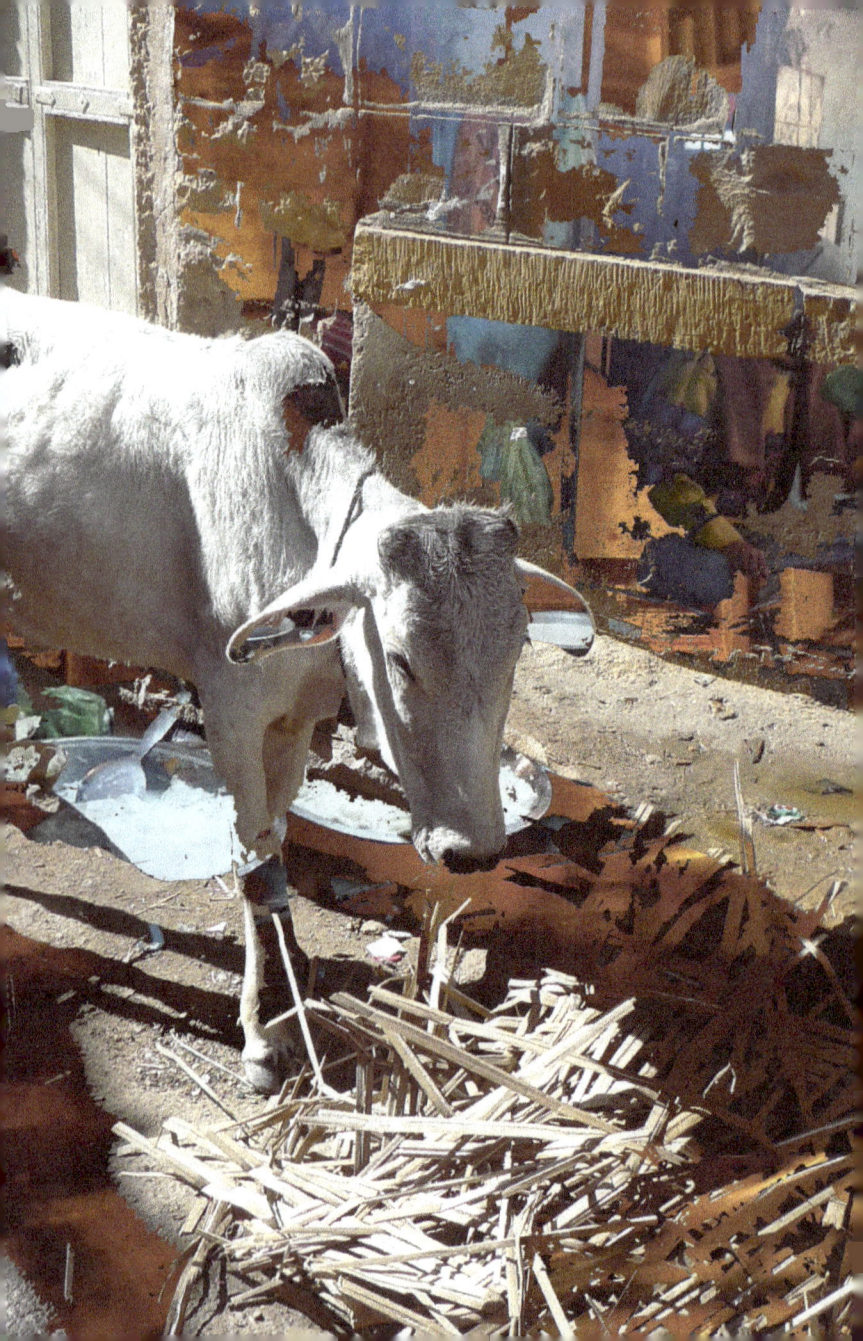

The Castle of Forbidden Language

Lays bare all its fruit.

The Castle of Public Knowledge

A second-hand drawbridge and an empty moat.

ALL ROADS
LEAD TO LHASA

All the motes of dust
encircled us like stars.

Part One
{Plastique}

I.

The Tai Pan Chinese Restaurant Behind Rosemont

1.

During the day, the ants can be seen skirting the windows and plaster molding—a long line handing off a relay of grains of salt and sugar, kernels of garlic and slivers of ginger. At night, behind, in the narrow alley, the cobbled street shimmers in peanut oil, or perhaps here in North America, it's canola. A giant vat of fat sweats, a swirl of effluents finds its way down the drain, along with the ducklings who play here in the shade—immigrants from across the other side of the park where by early morning, hecklers are plying their own sugary wares. Even in the breach there's nourishment.

2.

An old Asian man in breeches, an apron and an oily skull cap smokes a Panda cigarette, finds peace in the thrum of the ventilation, in the dancing, squeaking rats at lunchtime, the shades of plastic containers in the dumpster at midnight, or the occasional stray mutt who finds her way on all fours through the slop and grease only to discover an entire polystyrene container that snaps like shrimp crackers and oozes bacon and beef and rice with a dash of sesame and soy. Oh, what joy!

An old Asian man thinks the moon and stars are aligned: we are, of course, in the year of the dragon, and the dumplings this year have that hard chew.

3.

The interesting thing is this will all
vanish in an instant.

II.

Martha's Haberdashery
on Humboldt Circle Five

"Made to measure even if your children
outgrow them."

"Imagine your life in a year," the sign said.

"Which way will you grow," it said.

And so here we are, clamoring for our vanity, for all our buttons and bells and ribbons; clamoring for more-useless-or-less-is-more hanging in the windows. And yet, did you ever consider where the shirtless, trouserless, dressless button goes, into which treadmill it conspires to fasten itself in the gyre of here/not here. Not so for the burrs on which Velcro was modeled, they'll snag on any fair fur, and do their voodoo just like Mars, the cruel god of war who brings together the opposing poles of two lightning bolts. In the end they will all sink to the bottom of the ocean, and just like Fredericka and her trays full of beer at the Hofbraustube across the road, they will carry us over into the slop and splutter of other worlds.

III.

How To Skin a Weasel
Twenty-One Ways

Splayed

Behind the eyes,
Deep in there, look
For three streets
That divide the city,
Follow them all
In your dreams
Back to the source.
And by the source,
I mean where rivers
Arise, where oceans
Are but a thought
In a mind of water—

Water, water everywhere
And all those minute
Plastic micro-particles
Fused with the gut—
Hell, with the heart.

I don't have a heart
To tell him, do you?

Constrained

Constipated.
No shorter
Answer.

What was it
My sister said?
Meta-

Mucil works
A treat, or the
Fuzzy fibrous

Qualities of bran,
But for now,
Let me

Pour you
A jigger of
Grandpa's best.

Folding & Unfolding

A pastiche
At best, an
Origami

Steamcloud
That contains
A little *jois*

De vivre, some
Je ne sais
Quoi, or come

To that, some-
Thing more
Like a hairless

Cat upriver,
Lapping
It all up.

Wednesday Morning

Spring cleaning.
Steeplechasing.

Eternally
Philosophizing.

A solipsist
By any degree.

At least so said
My mother

In that very same tone
When you hadn't eaten

Your beans (or peas).
Remember all those nights

Under the halogen lights
That flickering-clicking

That never quite
Comes into being.

Bespoke Corduroy

"Love these tiny
Little stitches," she said,
Poking them. "Loved
Watching them
Flicker under the
Arc de Triomphe,
Looking for an angle."

Today's Thursday,
So we've no time
For the brass wire
And tacks. Please allow
For inclement weather.

To Be Outdone

Hell of a ride, this one. I thought you had forsaken me. All those difficult words. You said, "Salt, like meat, is a difficult commodity to sell." "Don't show the blood," you said, "and make sure it's kosher or halal. Better yet, make sure it's vegan or at the very least, behind the flock in all their mossy pastures."

A Primal Response

"Let me hand in my keys," she said.

"You never let me explain my story," she said.

"'Tis true," I said, setting myself up for the fall.

"And so, you admit it," she said.

"When we're done with this, I'm on my way home," I said.

"Quite typical," she said.

Have a Dram on Me

"There are no real distances," she said, "every atom is connected to the next. That is what makes me a creature—the worlds within worlds of the body, like the sun, like almonds."

And her body too leapt high among the angels on the ceiling and the flutes and the trumpets in all the corners of the sky.

Forgive Me

"For being me," she said.

"All the words in the world could never explain me,"
she said.

I said, "Surely one word—or two, is enough."

"Enough of that," she said stretching her toes over the
edge of the armchair, hair in curls, just out of the show-
er and smelling of roses.

I knew she meant what she said even when the sun
streamed in through the window and all the motes of
dust encircled us like stars.

A Sun in Any Another Galaxy

Halfway here nor there,
For half a moment, amazed

At night, knowing
All space is mysterious,

A downward trend all right.

Just a few more seconds ...

And the sun will implode.

Always in the City

It was established long ago that everything is magically nascent, fluttering, evanescent. Just check the writing on the wall of the toilet. It speaks to you and me, and reeks of discontent, malcontent, irreverence. But, just draw yourself a long bath and luxuriate in the suds that will one day reach the sea and wipe out coral reefs.

A Number

Happily discarded.

Fly in the Ointment

The drama soon commences, and thus the show begins.

"Aren't all gods lazy?" the choir bellows;

and yet there is this one voice that somehow coasts ahead, a skipping stone on a sound.

It is over and under the question;

Oh, these breakneck musical turns, the escargot on the flagpole, the crow in your ear, the hedgehog in your hair.

Upturned

High up on a mountain called Midnight, we chain our arms together.

Someone pours sand into a small bucket.

"How indulgent," says one.

"The sifting or shifting shall be eternally symbolized in that very last grain," says another.

"Every last grain," says she, dying.

Greasy Holy Water

The dark spaces
Only have a measure
Or an order
Having washed up here
Sometime in the future.

Undisturbed

That floating sound in the walls of my house
Where my birth was carved in stone.

It was the builders, not the prophets,
Who flooded the world with their spaces.

Watch the mouse navigate the lintel and the linen,
Skipping between knots of wood, through

The floor and into the walls of my house.

On the Order of Twelve Dozen

Cast in their shells, a hunter of feelings,
A purveyor of aphrodisiacs, or as they said
In the old days, a maker of fortunes.

A wise woman once told me each dozen
Constituted a parade of tears, a scattering
Of kisses and condolences like leaves

On a mound of snow; but then she asked
What was truly your bewildered moment, "Imagine,"
said she, "a dog comes upon
a mouse—bewilderment turns

to excitement quickly. Or do you play solely
for the benefit of the crows?"

On the Deck of an Ocean Liner

See how you flower,
Puffing up in great balls
Of flimsy skin, krill-like,
Catching the wind

As its own ocean;

And as in the deep—
so I imagine,
They have said that one day,
the world will absorb us.

They are wrong.

From the Armchair

The breath
Was smooth.
My heart was
Shaking against
The wind.

What you
Want to do
Is scatter pollen
Or you dry up
And go sour.

Look up, Flower,
Tighten your
Calf muscles,
And from
The shadows
The smell of piss
And mint will
Carry you, smooth.

After the Age of Innocence

Do you imagine
You really see me?

My old instrument is well
Aware of the contours

Of your hand. All that tissue
And bone, all that

Fissure and fizzle,
The lines drawn,

If in a circle, will
Return in the contours

Of the cell, all that
Separates matter

From the band
And their careening

Crooner in his
Cloak of invisibility.

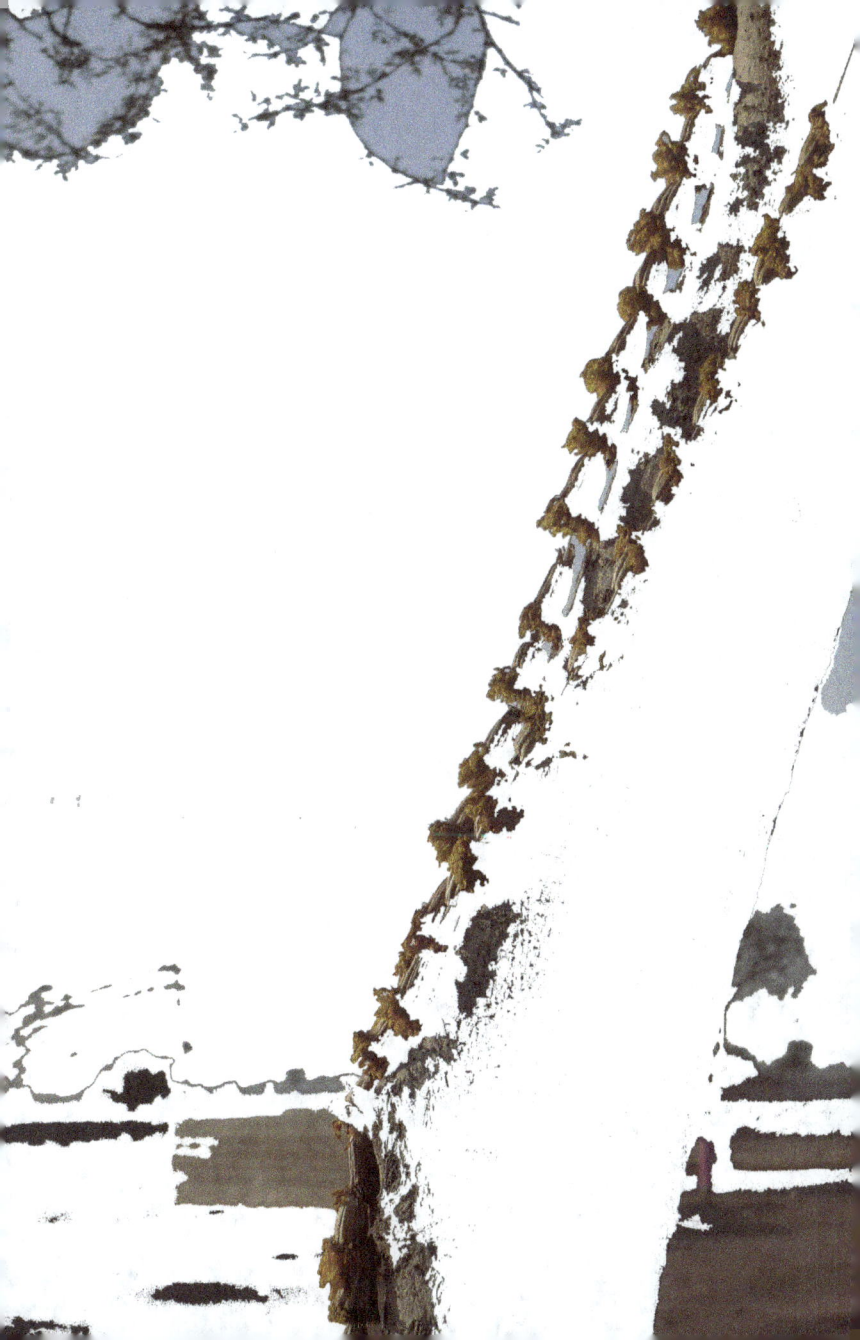

After the Tea Party

In an age of invisibility
We stride out toward the dawn,

Seeking all known forms:
Bakers, undertakers, chartered surveyors,

Citizens who punch holes, denizens
Of injection molders, the bipolar,

The maladjusted, they-who-creep-out-
Under-a-faint-lamplight, the drifters,

Sifters, layers of layers of plankton,
Fungal spores, daily chores, stifled

In the closet or the laundry room,
Tethered to the kitchen, the bed, the multi-

Form—all these contours, uncountably
Punctually held in shape by years

Of that nautilus on a platform: pelagic,
Jurassic, Cretaceous, Triassic, undeniably uni-

form.

Part Two
{All These Flat Surfaces}

≈

≈

A lizard, a Spanish gecko, dances across the ceiling. How does it feel to be upside down all the time? Why don't you pop a moth or two, then contemplate quantum time. And in line with the proscribed procedures pursuant to the Geneva Convention, and each anterior too, the concord of this and that, the dividing line between once-was-then-there-was-before. How does it feel to be upside down all the time?

At night, a barn owl makes her move, casting out, flying low—you see how her feathers bunch together when she goes in for the kill. Woe to be a lemming or a vole—once we were. Behind the wall they do it another way, they say, "What's in a lizard to you?" in their coy way.

≈

Follow the Spanish dancer down the street in the moonlight. Don't you see, anything can explode like a star.

≈

In between the hours of writing and reading comes music, the film, then that thrill of the chase, if the moon will. Or in another way, over the hill, in greener pastures, circling the mounds of the ancestors; and at any open gate you stare down inside the compound looking for what?—your soul? Another side of the lizard from the belly upward is that instinctual thing that guides you toward the light.

≈

The rush of bodies down in the latter half of town all consuming their dreams for a penny or two; and over there, at the Chinese takeaway, his hands full of trinkets, a detective slurps sesame noodles, a postman wipes his hands, a prosecuting attorney defends his Chop Suey, his choice of sauces; and over there at the sushi bar, a game keeper and her friends divide a single portion of California Rolls with extra wasabi—don't hold on the mayonnaise—and under the awnings in hermetically sealed containers, precisely where we sip coffee, a lizard cools himself in the shade. At night the spiders come out to spin their webs of intrigue, the moths and flies drawn to the light, to the flickering phosphor, to the warmed walls of humanity scattered everywhere. That's why the lizard won't budge a hair.

≈

And did I mention the raccoons emerging from their overhead lairs, dancing, late at night or early in the morning, feasting on sticky rice and flecks of ground pork and popcorn, on peanuts, on the dregs of the policeman's coffee, on the styrene spun into a flip-top, handy resalable containers. And watch the mother file in with her kids in an orderly row, through the bathroom window which was so conveniently held ajar the night before by a wad of doublemint gum. Just like us, they like things in straight lines, coordinated and color-coded. As a matter of moral philosophy, I generally take these things personally. I like to live up to all my expectations.

On a Beach Somewhere in Tibet

Stroking themselves in suntan lotion, in hand-
Fulls of will, gas filling the mouth cavity.

Ahead, the melting penumbra, the baptism

Of breath. An unknown presence makes
Himself known, not out of the sand, but

The air. His hairless calf muscles flex. The word

Obscure comes to mind, not hexed, not tongue-
Tied. He walks through the bottlecaps, through

The random flecks of silver and gold, through

The trodden sand, across the pylon and through
That fine mesh of lonley wires that is so casually

Draped across the balustrade of the pier.

Gulls call the shots here—oh, and the Land Rovers,
Muzzle to rear lining this wild frontier, this

Land of misbegotten souls. How would a Coke

Bottle from the sundrenched shores
Of the Yarlung Zangbo look

If landed here all awash in suntan lotion?

A Primitive State

How do you meet your death?
The derangements needed, all the guilty headed

Deep into their grammar, a primitive state—
And all the dinner parties, the no-room-available,

The stubborn who would have changed
Their names

For another set of teeth.

A Less Primitive State

Everything flows from here.
All these pronouncements

Made in the name of
The King, the generous

Pardons, the holier-
Than-thou meals and

The affairs of heads of state.
So you see that squirrel there?

Well let me tell you
She has survived the apoc-

Alypse seven times and
Still she gathers nuts.

World War Two

Don't forget where you came from or who you listen to, my grandmother said, cradling her own ginger cat staring out the window. As if its importance superseded everything else. I knew she didn't want me to listen to my old man; she had a big scheme in mind when she laid out the tea table at quarter past five—all those scones and crumpets, Grandfa hanging in the door. You could tell by the newspaper in the crook of his arm it was crossword time; but later, in the garden, in the woods at the back of the house, the daily bonfire with a dram of Gaelic whiskey that filled the Anglo-Saxon heart. And the birds in the trees went silent when he spoke, at least, so it seemed to me. Each word was weighed or weighted like plum lines that wound up a clock. And he would hover there, overlooking the crackling flames, the twigs and leaves snapping as a storm brewed. We burn all our excesses away, he would say, stroking his chin or wiping his glasses.

Imagining a Dystopian Future

Doubtlessly dying: A lone rock in imagined space,
A collection of words, an uplifting truth in serum,
A biological cocktail. Slight shift and every-
Thing changes. The locals go quiet in the pub,

Simply sipping their rum and cokes; Spanish blue fades
to continental grey. Eternal moments are im-
Agined more than lives ad infinitum. "Haul your
Arse out here," Uncle George would say in his
Crisp gray suit, suiting himself to my aunt Dorothy.

And all the Christmas cards thrown away,
The hundred images of folklore and mythology—
They were four-armed too, just like good old Ganesha
Cruising Tagore Street somewhere in Varanasi;

And the pyres and the effigies burning, the fumes
Alighting the light evening of scented candles and
Cheap perfume. "Wash your feet," the naked man
Covered up by his beard said. "Everywhere you walk

You cast dirty shadows. Make them clean."
Doubtlessly dying: the black hole is singing.

Only its back is visible.

Eye-Roll

Don't push too hard, they said. It will cost
Exorbitant calories—not that I'm saying you need

To lose some weight, not at all. Just remember
Everyone's fate is intertwined in the other half

Of mankind, those know-it-alls. In this state
We're reduced to our own roll-call. Live in

The meter, they said, even though we're all
Imperial, caught up in miles and inches, suffering

The near-deadly fall from a branch in a tree,

Which, if you've any bearing at all, means
The same as if you were never here.

Something Else Emerges
from the Primordial Soup

You know how they say everything is first divergent, before heading toward symmetry, toward their clean clear lives of delimitation; and despite that, all the world thrives on chaos, on the wild charades of tyrants and despots.

You know what? We're shifting the blame, setting course for Mars or the Hebrides, depending which is further apart; always something else: a doctor of philosophy, a shaman, a master or guru, you acolyte, you. I'm merely the way I am, you say, tugging your earlobe.

Sometimes I hear that cat scratching between the walls.

Who knows how she manages that?

Acknowledgements and Notes

"Imagining a Dystopian Future," made its first appearance in *The American Journal of Poetry*.

"≈ a lizard a Spanish gecko dances ...," reared its head in *Hanging Loose Journal*.

"A Primitive State" and "A Less Primitive State" peered into *Poetry Salzburg Review*.

"The Cartographer" and "Artificial Intelligence" peeked in on the *Fortnightly Review*.

"Alternate Worlds," arose blushingly in *Black Sun Lit*.

"An Empire in the Ground," whirled and danced into *The Common*.

"After the Age of Innocence" and "An Epitaph for Someone Alone in the Ground" soared into *Unlikely Stories*.

"A Number" appeared in *Boog City*.

"The Cartographer" is for my mother's father, Thomas Seach.

"A Primal Response" is for Dominique.

"Forgive Me," is for Iris.

www.ingramcontent.com/pod-product-compliance
Lightning Source LLC
Chambersburg PA
CBHW051002140626
46546CB00017B/2407